What
I See

What I See

A Collection of Poems

Norman Riggs Jr.

This book is a collection of poems.

Copyright © 2022 by Norman Riggs. All rights reserved.

The U.S. Copyright Act of 1976 protects this work; scanning, uploading, and digital sharing constitute intellectual property theft and illegal piracy.

Material from this book may be used for review purposes.

Published in the United States.

First edition (print & eBook): December 2022

ISBN: 9798370599637

*In memory of my father, Norman Riggs, Sr.,
my grandmother, Marie Porter, and
my beloved cousin Ahmad Harris*

Contents

Confused by Blue | 1
Just Like Me | 3
Kings We Are | 4
Light | 6
I Am Me | 8
I Want to Believe | 10
A Daily Thought | 12
Just Listen | 13
Then and Now | 14
Understanding and Hope | 16
My Morning Prayer | 17
Time | 19
Second Chance | 21
Pain and Faith | 23
Just for You | 25
What I See | 27
I Come to You | 29
Acknowledgements | 31
About the Author | 32

Confused by Blue

When I was younger,
I thought protecting and helping me
You was required to do.
Time passed. I've gotten a lot wiser.

Realized I had misconception of you.
I thought when emergencies occur,
I could definitely call on you,
Another mistake I made,
Thinking I could simply count on you.

You treat me with so much hate,
And such a high level of disrespect.
You start to gather,
Around your brothers and sisters
Turning their heads,
Showing their own neglect.
In your eyes,
I'm either a threat or a suspect.

The statements in your reports,
Filled with out-right blatant lies.
The charges against you,
Seem to be a lesser charge,
Or either justified.

Hunting season seems all year round,
When it comes to taking
Our lives.
It's a repeat offense.
With very little or no consequence.

Protected by your uniform,
The system and your badge,
Demanding equal justice,
Is that too much to ask?

Attending another home-goin'
Once again on your behalf.

How can I distinguish
The good from bad?
There's no type of sign, patch,
Wristband, or halo over your head.
There may be a level of respect
From some of you.
But who can I trust?
I don't know who is who.
Maybe now you understand,
Why I'm confused by blue.

Just Like Me

You don't like the color of my skin
But you wanna look like me.
You don't like the way I wear my hair
But you wear yours like me.

You don't like the way I dress
But you dress like me.
You don't like the way I speak
But at times you sound like me.

You don't like when I stand-up for my beliefs,
You call it untasteful and disrespectful.
When you stand-up for your beliefs,
You call it patriotic and respectful.

You may not understand me.
You may never love me. You may never accept me.
I understand that you struggle with what you see in
    me. You love my culture. You just don't like me.

No matter your reason, or what you may think, In
    reality, you could never be just like me.

Kings We Are

I'm finding it hard to understand
And even harder to comprehend,
Why we are spending so much time
Destroying each other.

From strangers to kinfolk to friends.
It can't be by mistake,
It keeps happening time and time again.
I see the loss it's overwhelming,
But nowhere do I ever see the win.

Claiming stock on that block,
Willing to die like it's yours,
Are you willing to love,
And defend your family,
With that same type of sword?

We've been labeled, we've been judged,
As hoodlums, thieves, and thugs.
We are better than the above.

Kings we are.
Descendants from generations
And generations of kings.
The ingredient is not violence
But total unity.

Stop being adversaries. Become allies,
Build our communities. Build up your pride.
Protecting our own,
Preserving lives.

We need to teach our younger ones.
But before we can teach them,
We must learn ourselves.
Self-destruction is something
That must be taken off the shelf.

Light

I have experienced some ups,
Have seen my share of downs,
Have had plenty of laughter,
At times I have cried so loud,

Didn't even make a sound.

Have celebrated with others,
Their joy and success
Never once did I forget
How much I have been blessed.

I have traveled those roads
Of uncertainty, confusion, and doubt.
Forgetting for a moment,
All I had to do,
Take the time to reach out.

Having to learn to take
The good with the bad,
The crooked with the straight.
Had to learn to enjoy this life
And never lose my faith.

Along with the many blessings
There has been some sacrifice.
No matter the darkness
There has always been light.
Thinking about the pain that
I have felt in my life.

I Am Me

I am in no way bound by
Your feelings and actions.
I am the pillar
On which you lean.
I possess the path
On which you follow.
A unique figure with no dimensions.
An outstanding creation
With great intentions.

Could I be that delight
You envision in your life?
One that leaves your heart and soul,
Full of curiosity and temptation?
Or could I just be
A figment of your imagination?

Capturing your days,
Mesmerizing your nights,
Always in reach,
But never in sight,
Like ole man river,
Moving along,
Never still, but never gone.
I am as big as you think,
As smart as you think,
As beautiful as you think.

I am me.

I Want to Believe

I want to believe,
A change a change will happen.
As decades pass
The outcome's the same.

One country, two sets of laws.
We march
We protest
We speak our minds.

Liberty and justice for all.
Liberty and justice for all.
Liberty and justice for all.
Do these words apply to me?

I just don't see.
I want to believe,
A change is gonna come,
Where we can live and love
And be together as one.

But the power of hatred
Continues to live on.
I want to believe
A change is gonna come.

I believe I can be part of the change,
If I am blessed to live long enough.

A Daily Thought

It has been said before
It is best to leave your past behind.
I like to carry my past
Right by my side.
My past defines
Who I have become.
How you deal with your past
Is for you to decide.
You may never touch
A million dollars,
But maybe you can touch
A million lives.

Just Listen

We need injustice and racism to cease,
Equality to increase,
That's why there's protest, marches, and taking a knee,
Has nothing to do with disrespect,
For the flag or the military.

Will the circle of equality,
Ever be complete?
Could you endure this same injustice,
If you were me?
Your perception is only what you see,
By you not listening,
Is why you don't hear me.

Then and Now

Emotions of emptiness at times arise,
Then there are times I think of every one of you and
I possess nothing but a smile.
Teaching me to be a great person, even a better man,
Didn't quite understand.
I never knew. I was just a kid.

Sit up straight, hold your head high
When speaking to someone,
Look them straight in the eye.
Taught me who I am, taught me how to
Never be ashamed of your skin.
Didn't quite understand,
Never knew, being a kid,

Keep faith in the Lord,
He will always be there for you.
Thank him often and over again,
Didn't quite understand,
Never knew, being a kid.

Treat others the way you want to be treated.
Embrace everyone with respect.
Yes sir, yes ma'am,
Was part of that concept.
Never knew, being a kid.
Didn't quite understand,
You all was molding me to become,
The man that I am.

Understanding and Hope

I am aware one day,
I will leave this earth,
The only sure occurrence
That is accompanied by birth.

I don't know how,
No idea where or when,
Something I graciously accept,
Having no fear in leaving here.

Maybe a burning building,
A fatal crash or accident
Or even natural causes,
Different situations how life has its losses.

Understanding and willing,
To accept all of that,
I don't want to die,
Just because I am black.

My Morning Prayer

I come to you this morning,
Thanking you for this day,
As I do every day,
On my knees, bowing my head,
As I start to pray.

Today I come to you,
Ask nothing for myself.
I pray to you,
To bless family and friends,
With long life, happiness,
And good health.

Heal those that are ill,
Give strength to those that are weak,
May the homeless receive
Shelter and warmth,
And plenty of meals to eat.
Please bless us Lord,
All with world peace.

For all the blessings,
You have cast upon me,
Throughout the years.
I say thank you once again,
I love you so deeply,
I owe it all to you,
Thank you, Lord. Amen.

Time

Sometimes I feel weak,
At times a bit weary,
Thoughts I have had before,
So frightening and scary.

There have been many days,
The burden seemed so heavy,
Like drowning in water over your head,
On a snowy hilltop,
On a runaway sled.

From pebbles, rocks, to boulders,
This weight continues,
Sitting on my shoulders.
The smiles and laughter,
Worn on the outside,
Hides the hurt that resides inside.

What you don't see is that
I am tired.
It doesn't make it any easier,
Have ventured this journey before,
If I possessed the strength I had
I could do a little more.

It's time to turn these battles over,
Been up against some stressful fights,
The time has come to sit back now
And evaluate my life.

Second Chance

Looking down on the city,
Sitting high on a hilltop,
Thinking of my life,
And all that's come about.

Never thought it would get to this point.
This all seems so unreal.
Bewildered and depressed
Sitting on this here hill.
Feeling empty and hurt inside,
All I seem to do,
Drop my head in my hands
And begin to cry.
These feelings feel so uncontrollable,
For reasons I don't know why.

Knowing I am stronger than these thoughts,
Yet I feel discouraged, stressed, and awfully weak.
Hard to understand these feelings,
I just want to be at peace.
Sitting here on this hill,
Thinking this would be so much easier,
That's just the way, I had it figured.

Pulled out a gun.
Raised it to my head.
Then I pulled the trigger.

Something happened,
Nothing happened.
It never went off.
I cried out so loud,
Asked for forgiveness,
As I sat on that hilltop.

A voice came out to me,
I forgive you my child,
I understand,
I have more for you to do,

Put your trust, faith
And love in me,
I will help you through.
Never will I forsake you,
I will forever be here for you.

Reach out to me,
Trust in me,
Come and take my hand,
I have blessed you my child,
You have a second chance.

Pain and Faith

Pain seems over-whelming,
And at times everlasting,
Seeking and searching,
Finding no understanding.
The hurt overbearing.

Pain is deep
Leaving you weary, drained, and weak.
Closing your eyes,
Finding it hard to sleep.
Even at times
Finding no urge
Or appetite to eat.

As you lay there you start to cry
Over and over again.
You keep asking yourself why.
As the tears continue
To flow from your eyes,
From all the confusion
Going on inside your heart,
And within your mind.

Hard to believe all this pain
Will heal in time,
With faith, love, and trust in God,
I know you'll be just fine.

Just for You

In Memory of James T. "Mr. A" Aglamesis

Thinking of you,
Starting to reminisce,
Things that come to mind,
I will truly miss.

Your genuine passionate heart,
Warm, soothing and so kind,
I will forever remember
That caring and loving smile.

You offered so much kindness,
Throughout your wonderful life,
From the conversations, encouragement,
Life lessons and all your good advice.
You will never be forgotten,
Always and forever will be missed,
Memories of you bring us all,
Comfort, love, laughter and happiness.

Those moments will occur,
We may even shed some tears,
But in the end,
We thank God,
For loaning you to us,
For all these many years.

What I See

In my mind I visualize,
This is what I see.
A place where people are not divided,
By skin color,
Political or religious beliefs.
An atmosphere full of love, life
And everlasting peace,
No hatred, homeless, sickness, wars,
Prejudice or poverty.

I see exotic plants,
Rows of beautiful flowers,
Time does not matter,
Not one second, one minute,
Not one passing hour.
The skies appear so magical,
So beautiful and blue,
And countless colorful rainbows,
I visualize too.

A place to reunite,
With family and friends,
All of those you thought about,
And missed throughout the years.
Since heaven has no visiting hours,
This is what I see.
When my time comes to leave,
All I ask, dear Lord,
Please save a place for me.

I Come to You

My Heavenly Father,
I come to you bowing my head,
Down on bending knees,
Lead us, cover us,
You are truly what we need.
Father we are divided by
Hatred, racism, insecurities, and false beliefs.
If we believe in you,
How could this be possible?
I stand by you, I walk with you,
In you I do believe.

As I come to you,
With tears in my eyes,
My heart bleeds,
Parents burying their kids,
Not the way it's supposed to be,
Mass killings are destroying us,
Much like a fatal disease,
Father as I pray to you,
Please hear my plea.

You created something beautiful and pure,
But destruction is all I see,
Father cover us, heal us, lead us,
I come to you once again,
Down on bended knees.

Acknowledgements

All praises to God who makes all things possible.

To the Riggs, Rowles, Harris, Plair, Essex, Judon, Smoot, Thomas and Gates families. Thank you for your love and support.

A special thank you to Jamie Flerlage and Patti Normile.

About the Author

Norman Riggs, Jr., is the author of *Lil of a Lot: A Collection of Poems*, published in June 2020. He enjoys walks in the park, jazz, sports, and following his favorite National Football League team, the Cleveland Browns. Riggs is at work on his next collection of poems. He may be reached at normanriggs6@gmail.com.